BARREN ROAD

BARREN ROAD

POEMS

J.R. SOLONCHE

SERVING HOUSE BOOKS

Barren Road
Copyright © 2025 J.R. Solonche
First Edition

All rights reserved. No part of this book may be reproduced or transmitted in any form or by any means, electronic, digital, or mechanical, including photocopy, audio recording, or any information storage and retrieval system, without prior permission from the publisher or author (except by reviewers who may quote brief passages).

Front cover art by J.R. Solonche
Cover design by Jacob Arms

Published by Serving House Books
Lawrence Landing Company
Raleigh, North Carolina 27609
United States of America

www.servinghousebooks.com

Serving House Books is a proud member of

Independent Book Publishers Association
 and
Community of Literary Magazines and Presses

Paperback ISBN: 978-1-947175-78-5

Library of Congress Control Number: 2025936593

SERVING HOUSE BOOKS

Praise for J.R. Solonche

"Solonche is productive and prolific, but that doesn't water down his poetry... He can compress a philosophical treatise into three lines... His epigrammatic tidy poems are philosophic gems. Solonche sees humor and encapsulates it; he frames a thought in perfect verse... He's playful and profound — the more he writes, the more he seems to know. Beneath the Solonche simplicity are significant social comments, and his goodwill reinforces the best in us."

—Grace Cavalieri,
Washington Independent Review of Books

"Solonche, an accomplished poet, employs various forms in this compilation, including haiku, prose poem, and free verse. The poems often imaginatively enter into the natural or material world via anthropomorphic similes... Many works have an aphoristic quality that recall Zen koans, and they can be playfully amusing or even silly... A strong set of sympathetic but never sentimental observations."

—*Kirkus Reviews*

"The tone is established from the outset: wry, wise, sardonic and playful, drawing the reader irresistibly in. Solonche is revealed as a philosopher in the mold of Wittgenstein: aphoristic, charismatic, acerbic and oddly mystical. If you met this book in a bar, you would definitely want to take it home with you and every day thereafter congratulate yourself on how lucky you've been. But that is true of all his books."

—David Mark Williams

Table of Contents

Barren Road	1
Nothing to Speak Of	2
Found Poem	3
Dementia	4
Pocket Wash	5
The Air Is Still	6
Forsythia	7
The Change	8
Short April Pastoral	9
Conversation on Easter at Easter	10
Mountain Laurel	11
Wild Black Cherry	12
After the Reading	13
April Seventh	14
Eclipse	15
River Birch	16
Memorial Service for a Potter	17
Very Short April Pastoral	18
Cemetery	19
A Wind	20
O Lady	21
The Ides of April	22
The Trees	23
Awakening from Dreams	24
Fisherman	25
Petals	26
Hope	27
The Gymnast	28
First	29
The Dance	30
Shadows	31
For Me Spring Is Done	32
I Hear My Neighbor	33
Two Lakes	34
Dandelions	35

The Shadows of Dead Flowers	36
Cardinal	37
Poetry Contest	38
Birding	39
Skill	40
Boulder	41
I Miss the Lilacs	42
Crimson Azalea	43
Too Much Time Has Passed	44
Workshop	45
Two White Butterflies	46
Helen and Helen	47
Meditation	49
Kafka	50
Bird at an Empty Feeder	51
Perfection	52
Sometimes	53
Raleigh Wasn't Right	54
The Sky	55
The Road	56
The Past	57
At No One's Grave	58
"Beautiful Thing," You Said	59
Worm	60
Lilies	61
Dogwoods	62
Dance	63
A Game	64
Elegy for Victoria, 27	65
Old	66
Very Short May Pastoral	67
Sudden Shadow	68
Peony	69
The Moon	70
Dementia	71
Red-Tailed Hawk	72
Reading	73

Reflections	74
The Surprise	75
A Dandelion	76
It Was Dark	77
The Neighbor	78
Zhao Li Looks Up	79
Zhao Li Pauses to Watch	80
Zhao Li Stops by the Lake	81
Zhao Li Pauses in Front	82
Zhao Li Hears a Noise	83
Zhao Li Sees a Dragonfly	84
Zhao Li Pauses to Admire	85
Zhao Li Says Good Morning	86
The Angel	87
Money	88
For E.K.	89
An Irony	90
To My Daughter	91

BARREN ROAD

I have a friend who lives on Barren Road. It's a shame he's not a poet. "It's a shame you're not a poet," I said. "Why's that?" he said. "Because you live on Barren Road," I said. "So that's why it's a shame I'm not a poet?" he said. "Yeah. Consider the irony," I said. "I do. I've been considering it all the time since it really was barren," he said. "I'm surprised at you. This is the first time you said it's a shame I'm not a poet. Well, I think it's a shame you are. A damn shame. What a waste of a mind," he said. I understand. He's a sociologist.

NOTHING TO SPEAK OF

Nothing to speak of
save the crocus, white
here, purple there, no
yellow yet, but they will
show up, and oh yes,
plenty of daffodils in
their neat bunches in front
of my neighbor's house,
but I don't speak of them.

FOUND POEM
(OVERHEARD AT MY NEIGHBOR'S WAKE)

Sorry, dear,
I'm not
feeling
this funeral.

DEMENTIA

So you want to know what this sleep is?
What this dream is?
You must think of the first sleep
you slept out of the womb.
You must think of your dream of the womb.
If you cannot, you will not know this sleep.
If you cannot,
oh, my friends,
you will not know this dream.

POCKET WASH

He wrote a poem about a gold
pocket watch given to his uncle
by President Lyndon Johnson
for working to desegregate
schools in the south and then
passed down to him. It played
Hail to the Chief when opened.
But the editor of the magazine
titled the poem, *Pocket Wash*
in the Contents, and surely
washing the pocket is something
the nephew would never want
to do after his uncle's pants
held that pocket watch from
President Lyndon Johnson for
all those years in the closet.

THE AIR IS STILL

The air is still,
so still, one doubts
that it is even air
except that it can be
breathed in and held
and breathed out again
into the very spot it had been.

FORSYTHIA

Leaving this overcast,
dark gray, rainy morning,
I heard the forsythia at
the bottom of the driveway
shout, "We blackmailed the sun
to be this sun-golden, so
do not forget this when you get
back, and it is here this afternoon."

THE CHANGE

How quick is the change.
Not a moment is wasted,
not an instant of sun not taken,
not a single degree unused,
how can we say *Already*
to these who have been
ready so long?

SHORT APRIL PASTORAL

The wind is winter's unfinished business.
The shoots of the lilies pay it no mind.

Soon we will know which trees are dead, which alive.
Soon the grass will cleanse our minds of snow.

The tallest trees make the best dancers.
Even the dead trees dance joyously.

The daffodils hog the yellow.
They have no need to dance, but they do.

CONVERSATION ON EASTER AT EASTER

I asked him about suffering.
He said that philosophers
have struggled over it for
centuries. I asked him again
about suffering. He said that
it is needed for redemption.
I asked him again about
suffering. He said that men
bring it on themselves.
I stopped asking him about
suffering, for I saw that
he was suffering enough.

MOUNTAIN LAUREL

You are old now,
Old Mountain Man,
and you are tall now, too,
taller than I am,
and your small white
flowers fall in
foamy splashes of spittle
down your long bony legs.

WILD BLACK CHERRY

So here we are again,
white-haired old man,
sharing another spring.
Oh, with no other than
you would I share this
or any spring, or any winter,
or any promise, or any betrayal.

AFTER THE READING

After the reading, the poet was asked,
"Why do you write?" "I write because
the silence is too much to bear," he answered.
I hope someone asks me the same question,
for I shall answer, "I write because the noise
is too much to bear."

APRIL SEVENTH

When I come back
in my next life, if
there is a next life,
I want to come back
as these honey bees
in the wild black cherry.
Yes, you heard me right.
Not as a single honey bee.
As all of the honey bees.

ECLIPSE

The astronomer said
that it's just a coincidence
that the sun is 400 times
the size of the moon
and that the moon is 400
times nearer the earth,
which is why one overlays
the other so perfectly, but
I say it is no coincidence,
for I have had a dream
that told me so.

RIVER BIRCH

My neighbor has a river
birch in his yard. It is old
and fully grown, twenty
feet or more, but still has
the tag from the nursery
tied to the trunk. I looked
at it out of curiosity. Among
other advice, like lots of sun
and ample watering, it says to
plant two at a time. I see no
evidence of a companion tree.
He may have planted two.
One may have died, so he may
have cut it down. And maybe
the grass overgrew that spot.
But I tend to believe he never
planted two to begin with. As
I say, it's alive, but it's such a sad
looking thing, lonely and sad,
so I'm thinking I'll go buy a young
healthy river birch, sneak into
his yard in the dark of night, dig
a hole, and plant it next to the old
one. Then I'll say a prayer that
it's not too late. It's the least I can
do for the sad lonely old river birch
in my neighbor's yard. I hate sadness.
I hate loneliness. I hate them.

MEMORIAL SERVICE FOR A POTTER

Your spirit was there with us he said.
And I agree that your spirit was there with us
as the spirit of the departed is always there with them.
But where exactly was that I wondered.
Was your spirit in the bumblebee
bumping around the tent?
Was your spirit in the woodpecker
hammering overhead?
Was your spirit in the river below us
beyond the railroad tracks?
Was your spirit in the big black beetle
crawling on his shoulder
while he was bragging that he was chosen
because he was the only one
who could do it without weeping?
Tell the truth.
Wasn't your spirit in the ceramic cup you made,
the one that leaked white wine on his lap
because he bragged he could do it without weeping?

VERY SHORT APRIL PASTORAL

My neighbor's saw
is sing-
ing a circular song of spring!

CEMETERY

It is old enough to make unreadable the oldest stone.
Soon it will no longer even be a cemetery.
What does soon mean?
Soon means when the iron fence
is rusted totally away.
Soon means when the thick brambles
forbid you visitation there.
Soon means when it is out of sight.
Soon means when it is out of mind.

A WIND

A wind neither too gentle
nor too strong, but a wind
just right to blow the cherry
blossom petals from the cherry tree
on the other side of the house
over the roof has done just that.

O LADY

O Lady, married
as we are to others,

yet we touch
each other,

today on the hand,
tonight on the heart,

so far away,
from each other, so far apart.

O Lady, with eyes
as blue as the sky

and just as far beyond
both me and your eyes,

I am in that
same awful Nowhere.

THE IDES OF APRIL

The earth is
executing flowers
today, so Beware!
Beware of the Beauty!

THE TREES

The tree I a year ago
thought dead is alive.

The tree I a year ago
thought alive is dead.

This may be the best of
all reasons to stop thinking.

AWAKENING FROM DREAMS

It takes longer now.
It takes more sun at the window.
It takes the sun longer at the window now.
My dreams are stronger.
They are stronger than the world.
They are better than the world.
When I awaken from dreams,
I fall into a dreamless sleep.

FISHERMAN

I was never a fisherman
although I lived on a lake,
and I had a small boat,
and I had a rod and a reel
and a net, and I caught
a bass or two, and threw
them back, but I was never
a fisherman. I'm not sure
what it would have taken.

PETALS

They will leave
no trace when
the leaves replace
them except, far
down in the earth,
in the roots, they, too,
will take root and wait.

HOPE

Not an end in itself
but the means to an
end desired, like wings
or a woman's name.
Don't believe everything
you read. This is hope.
Just this.

THE GYMNAST

Virtuoso of the body,
she does with muscles
and tendons and bones
what the rest of us
can only do with our souls.

FIRST

The first butterfly I've seen
so far this spring flies
among the myrtle and the dandelions,
not stopping, not pausing, but
knowing that not these are the keys
to its chemical heart,
disappears behind the shed.

THE DANCE

The one red tulip
in the vase of daffodils
sticks out like a sore thumb
but nevertheless dances
the same dance in the wind.

SHADOWS

I am reading a poem
about an overcast day
in which the poet wrote,
"The day is overcast.
I cast no shadow, so
therefore I do not exist,"
and he was right, for
I, too, cast no shadow,
so I, too, do not exist.

FOR ME SPRING IS DONE

For me spring is done
when the trees leaf out,
and the last of the cherry
blossom petals have fallen
onto the driveway and
have disappeared from
the driveway. I know
what you will say. You
will say that spring is
just beginning then, but
for me this is when it is done.

I HEAR MY NEIGHBOR

I hear my neighbor
talking. I cannot make
out the words, so I do
not know what he is
talking about, but it is such
a low and friendly and civil
tone of voice, it can't be politics.

TWO LAKES

As lifeless as this page
on which nothing is yet
written, yet not dead
either, for life, so much life,
is stirring just beneath
the surface of the two lakes.

DANDELIONS

If they weren't yellow,
as bright and as yellow
as any daffodil, more so
than some daffodils,
I would mow them down
with the grass like grass.

THE SHADOWS OF DEAD FLOWERS

As far as their shadows
are concerned, these flowers
are still very much alive,
so I'll leave them in the sun longer,
where they belong.

CARDINAL

Scientists say that colors
do not exist.

Tell that to
the female cardinal.

POETRY CONTEST

I judged a poetry contest.
There were 71 poems by
students. The winning poem
was "The Holes in Notebooks."
It was written by a fifteen-
year old girl. I wept when
I read it at home. She wept
when she read it at the lectern.
For the first time in my life,
I wished I were sixteen again.

BIRDING

They are not for me
to identify. The birds
know who they are.
Let the birders boast
and brag and fill up
their books, those
books that should be
the first to burn.

SKULL

The landscaper found
a skull at the edge of
the woods. What is it?
I said. It looks like a cat,
he said. Oh, are you sure
it's not a possum or a skunk?
I said. No, I'm pretty sure
it's a cat, he said. I knew
he was right. I knew it was
a cat as soon as I saw it.
I knew it was Homer, and
I felt sick because I knew I
hadn't buried him deeply
enough, and I was hoping
it was a possum or a skunk,
and I felt sick that I had
not buried my cat properly.
What should I do with it?
he said. I don't know. I feel
sick, I said, walking back
to the house.

BOULDER

If stone could be lonely
when alone, surely this
boulder, the only one in
the company of the cut logs
beside the split-rail fence, would be.

I MISS THE LILACS

I miss the lilacs
that used to bloom in
the front yard.
I could smell them from
the doorstep as soon
as I opened the door.
One was white. The other
was lilac-colored. One
reminded me of Whitman,
the other of winter.

CRIMSON AZALEA

I wasn't expecting it anymore,
the crimson azalea about to burst
into flower now. It is old, and it
didn't flower last year. I considered
cutting it down, removing it, root
and all, but I was lazy, as I've always
been about such things, so I let it be.
Today I thank the goddess of azaleas
for stilling my hand against it,
thank her for this miracle of turning
bloody thoughts to flowers.

TOO MUCH TIME HAS PASSED

Too much time has passed.
I cannot think of starting over.
Too much time, O too much time
has passed over me to even think
of being so foolish, I, who have been
so good at being the fool.

WORKSHOP

He wrote a poem about ants.
It was bad. There were too
many ants. There are too many
ants, I said. What should I do?
he said. Rewrite the poem,
this time about one ant, I said.
So he rewrote the poem. It was
good. This is good. What did
you learn? I said. That too many
ants spoil the poem, he said.
Yes. You don't need to come here
anymore, I said.

TWO WHITE BUTTERFLIES

When are two butterflies
a pair of butterflies? These
seem still foreplaying out
and in the garden so not
yet a pair, yet they dance
to the push and pull of
chemistry's syncopation,
toward, away, away, and toward.

HELEN AND HELEN

Growing up I knew two Helens.
The first was Helen Green. Her
real name was Greenburg, but
her father changed it to Green.
He once wrote a letter to Hank
Greenburg castigating the great
ballplayer who was the frequent
target of anti-Semitic taunts from
fans and other players for not
changing his name to something
less Jewish. Helen lived in my
building, but we weren't friends.
She was smart and went to Hunter
High School. The other Helen was
Greek, Helen Kontos. She wasn't
smart. We went to the same high
school, but we weren't friends
either because she was beautiful.
Helen Kontos was so beautiful
I didn't have the nerve to say a
word to her. Besides, she was
going out with Ira Tartack, the
captain of the football team.
I thought that if there were
anything worth getting beaten
up for it would be Helen Kontos.
Anyway, as I said, she was Greek,
which didn't mean anything to
me until Mr. Feinberg, our senior
year English teacher had us read

The Iliad. "The Trojan War was
about a woman," he told us. "A
woman named Helen who was so
beautiful her face launched 1,000
ships." It made perfect sense.
I got an "A" in that class, my only
one. I never knew what became of
the beautiful Helen Kontos, but
I'm quite sure she married Ira,
had four or five kids and got fat.
I do know what happened to Helen
Green, the smart Helen. She became
the District Attorney of Bronx County,
the face that launched 1,000 prosecutions.

MEDITATION

Medication
is
more
like
it.

KAFKA

I wish we had lived at
the same time just long
enough to have shared
letters, one from me to
you, Franz, and one from
you to me. Only that long.

BIRD AT AN EMPTY FEEDER

Don't be dismayed, brother.
I'm the same way,
returning again and again
to the dried up well of expectation,
to the exhausted spring of the unlearned lesson.

PERFECTION

Do you know what
perfection is?

I don't either,
but I do like thinking

about not thinking
about what perfection is

as though I were
studying Zen Buddhism.

SOMETIMES

Sometimes you lose me,
Bill, as now, with
"Impromptu: The Suckers."
Of course, if anyone
could have pulled it off, it was you.
Nevertheless... Nevertheless...

RALEIGH WASN'T RIGHT

We can go to the country,
for the country will bring us peace.

Peace of a sort.
Peace of a kind.

A country kind of peace,
so much easier to know where

the birds are louder
than the buses and taxis.

Is it ideal?
Is it idyllic?

Not by a long shot.
But listen.

Do you not hear it?
The hummingbird now returning from Mexico?

THE SKY

There's not a cloud.
If I were to leap out into the sky,
what would I hold onto?
How would I keep myself from falling
back down to earth?

THE ROAD

I drive around the lake.
It's deserted.
No one is out on the water.
The roads, too, are empty.
I am alone on the road.
Soon, though, as if by magic,
the buses will appear.
They will be everywhere.
They will release the school children who will look like
butterflies emerging from orange cocoons.
I will stop for them.
I will watch the younger ones run
into the arms of the mothers
and the arms of the fathers.
I will watch the older ones bring the mail
from the mailboxes, sullenly, into the houses.

THE PAST

I wanted to
let it go,

but it beat
me to it

and let me
go before

I had
the chance.

AT NO ONE'S GRAVE

This ground is undisturbed.
Here no digging has been done.
But death has been here.
It still is here. It has always been here.
It will always be here. With life,
together, inseparable. They are identical twins.
One male, one female.
No. Both female.

"BEAUTIFUL THING!" YOU SAID

"Beautiful Thing!" you said,
many times. "Beautiful Thing!
Beautiful Thing!" May I borrow
it, Bill? Yes, I must borrow it.
I must have them for myself,
these words, these two beautiful
words for my own purposes,
my own beautiful thing to sing
about in my own time, with my
own harmonies, for so few, so
few beautiful things are there in
the world that we must share
them, all the few things beautiful
that are all the few joys forever!

WORM

A worm roams, twists forward
on the patio stones.
There is something heroic
about the way it struggles forward,
forward toward – What? –
a destination I cannot begin to fathom.
It cannot be some shelter from the sun,
for it would have found that in the deep cracks.
It cannot be food, for that it has ignored
on its tortured journey.
No, it must be something else
that the worm twists forward for.
Some genetic impulse propels it,
commands, "Forward, forward, forward, and die!"
As with all heroes.

LILIES

Matthew was so wrong.
Of course, they toil.
Of course, they spin.
They're alive aren't they?

DOGWOODS

White clouds
in a green sky,
but the dogwoods
look like winter,
which is the only
thing about them
I can do without.

DANCE

I have two left
feet, so I dance
out of both sides
of my mouth.

A GAME

Loud shouts at a game.
It does not matter
what. It is a game.
It is the home field.
The home team scores.
There are shouts.
The shouts are loud
from the field beyond
the trees as I go home
to my quiet house.

ELEGY FOR VICTORIA AGE 27

Victoria, how serious you were.
I never had such a serious student as you,
covered now by these years of this serious earth.
That time you saw me from the bus and crossed
over the Green, you wore such a serious smile,
right away I knew how it would have to be.
I would have to be serious, too, if I let it go on,
allowing my own serious smiles to grow into
love too serious for their casual campus
adulteries. No one would, no one could, possibly
understand. My colleagues? Never. They
rated their conquests, counted the coeds
enjoyed in their offices, under their desks.
No, Victoria, that wasn't me, and
how could it ever be you that way? Never.
Angry? I hope you are not angry with me,
resting now over these serious years,
resting as you will forever be resting.
I will love you, seriously, oh, seriously,
sweet Victoria, who I most seriously of all, sing for.

OLD

I know I am getting old.
Five pots for flowers
this year instead of eight.
Four types of flowers
in them instead of six.
Two whiskies at three
instead of three at five.
No women, no women,
no women instead of one.

VERY SHORT MAY PASTORAL

Three butterflies are still dancing
while the wooed still decides between them.

The peonies have reached their height.
Now it is all about weight.

So many birds in the woods all at once.
I hear them all but listen to the loudest.

SUDDEN SHADOW

Crow, you scorn
me unlike your cousin's
Samuel's, so caw everywhere,
and you will subdue
this blue air.

PEONY

Peony I plucked out
from the garden space
to put in this vase,
it's your fault for being first.

THE MOON

The morning
was hollow,

but the afternoon
filled it solid,

so night with its moon
will wait outside,

having no way in
until tomorrow.

DEMENTIA

"Does she still smile?"
her friend asked.
"Yes, she still smiles,"
I said. "I think she
will always smile,"
she said. "Yes, the doctor
thinks so, too, but the reasons
will change he said," I said.

RED-TAILED HAWK

He's so majestic up there
on the power lines
in his Imperial red,
it's a wonder the voles
and the field mice
are not queued up waiting
their turn to be sacrificed.

READING

I get up and
put my book
on the chair.
It's out of place,
yet how politely
it waits there.

REFLECTIONS

My reflection in
the window glass
is not how others
see me. It is how
I see myself as
others see me, thus
how I do not wish
to be seen at all.

THE SURPRISE

"I have a surprise for you,"
says the morning.
"I do not like surprises," I say.
"I have one anyway," says the morning.
"Fine. What is it?" I say.
"You are alive," says the morning.

A DANDELION

Zhao Li pauses in front
of a dandelion. "Why do
all my neighbors hate you
and your kind?" he asks.
"Your neighbors hate us
because we make them feel
guilty," says the dandelion.
"Oh, I understand. In that
case, I, too, would hate you,
but because you are welcome
at my home, I do not hate you,"
says Zhao Li going on his way.

IT WAS DARK

It was dark, as it should be,
under the weight of the clouds
and loud, as it should be, under
the thunder, but the rain was paltry,
a drizzle, whispers of drops
as though afraid of not living up
to its introduction.

MY NEIGHBOR

My neighbor doesn't
have a red wheelbarrow,
but he does have white
chickens upon which he
depends for eggs.

ZHAO LI LOOKS UP

at the sky, which is
flawless and blue.
"I know why you are
so blue, but how is it
that you are also so
flawless?" he says.
"Oh, I did not know I
was flawless. Neither
did I know I was blue.
Thank you for telling me,
Zhao Li," grins the sky.
"Oh, no, I fear I have made
a terrible mistake," Zhao
Li mumbles as he goes
on his way.

ZHAO LI PAUSES TO WATCH

the trees dance in the wind.
"The tallest trees make
the best dancers," he laughs.
"You said that the last time
you paused here to watch us
dance in the wind, Zhao Li,"
said the tallest trees. "Yes,
I did, and weren't you pleased
by my compliment?" Zhao Li
says. "Oh, yes, we were," say
the tallest trees. "So now I
compliment you a second time,
and for a second time are you
not pleased, for now you have
been complimented twice as
many times as I," says Zhao
Li as he continues on his way.

ZHAO LI STOPS BY THE LAKE

"It is a beautiful day, yet
there are no fishermen here.
Now were I a fisherman,
I would be baiting my hook
and casting my line," he says
aloud to himself. Suddenly,
a fish sticks its head up out
of the water. "Thank you for
not being a fisherman, Zhao
Li," says the fish. "Oh, you
mean you thank me for
sparing you the pain of
having a sharp hook in your
mouth?" Zhao Li says. "No,
I thank you for sparing me
the pain of having laughter
at you in my mouth," says
the fish as it disappears
under the water.

ZHAO LI PAUSES IN FRONT

of the hummingbird feeder
to look at the ruby-throated
hummingbird. "I see you are
not the hummingbird to whom
I said, *Adios, amigo,* a year ago.
Nevertheless, "Hola, camarada,
eres bienvenido aquí," says Zhao Li,
grateful to be able to practice his Spanish.

ZHAO LI HEARS A NOISE

so stops and turns,
but he sees no one.
"Oh, not yet, not yet,"
he says to the one who
is not behind him yet
and continues on his way.

ZHAO LI SEES A DRAGONFLY

fly by. "What's your hurry?" he says.
"What do you mean? What is this
word *hurry?* I am merely going
about my business. Why are you
standing still, Zhao Li?" says the
dragonfly. "What do you mean?
What is this word *still?* I am merely
going about my business," says Zhao Li
as he watches the dragonfly go about
its business disappearing.

ZHAO LI PAUSES TO ADMIRE

the three peony bushes.
"I am the most beautiful one,
so you must admire only me,"
says the magenta peony bush.
"I am the most beautiful one,
so you must admire only me,"
says the yellow peony bush.
"I am the most beautiful one,
so you must admire only me,"
says the white peony bush.
"I am glad I do not have to choose,
for I would have chosen the blue
peony bush in my mind," says
Zhao Li to himself as he admires
all three peony bushes equally.

ZHAO LI SAYS GOOD MORNING

to the crowd of daisies
by the road. "Good morning,
keep us company for a while,
Zhao Li," they shout. "No
thank you. You do not need
my company. There are enough
of you to keep yourselves
company," says Zhao Li. Soon
he sees a single daisy on the
other side of the road. "Good
morning. I see you are all by
yourself. Shall I keep you
company for a while?" he says.
"No thank you, Zhao Li. I do
not need your company. I am
quite happy to have this side
of the road all to myself," says
the daisy. "Ah, I understand.
And I am quite happy to have
both sides of the road all to
myself," laughs Zhao Li as
he goes on his way.

THE ANGEL

Such a beautiful woman
in the supermarket,
surely she was an angel.
You cannot blame me, for
she was from that angle.

MONEY

I like money.
Emily Dickinson is my favorite poet.
For $32.35 I bought her *Complete Poems*.
For $49.99 I bought her *Complete Letters*.
For $50 in gas I visited her home in Amherst, Massachusetts.
For $450,000 I could buy a lock of her hair on eBay.
I would like to if I had the money, the money I like.

FOR E.K.

She has an eye for eyes,
this young artist,
still a teenager,
but look here,
how the mouths leave
much to be desired.

AN IRONY

When I awake in the morning
and I do not remember
my dream, I say to myself,
"Ah, that dream was not worth
remembering." Yet when I awake
in the morning and I do remember
my dream, I also say to myself, "Ah,
this dream is not worth remembering."

TO MY DAUGHTER

I do not wish a grave,
but you may give me one
if you insist. I cannot
stop you, for I know how
last wishes are many times
ignored when the living
believe the dead ask too
much of them, or when
they ask much, much too little.

Books by J.R. Solonche

POETRY

Collected Short Poems
Night Visit
Then Morning
Reading Takuboku Ishikawa & Other Poems
The Architect's House
God
The Eglantine
Alone
The Dreams of the Gods
The Book of a Small Fisherman
Leda
It's about Time
Around Here
The Lost Notebook of Zhao Li
Coming To
Life-Size
The Five Notebooks of Zhao Li
Selected Poems 2002-2021
Years Later
The Dust
A Guide of the Perplexed
For All I Know
The Moon Is the Capital of the World
Piano Music
Enjoy Yourself
The Time of Your Life
The Porch Poems
To Say the Least
A Public Place
True Enough
If You Should See Me Walking on the Road
I, Emily Dickinson and Other Found Poems

The Jewish Dancing Master
Tomorrow, Today and Yesterday
In Short Order
Invisible
Heart's Content
Won't Be Long
Beautiful Day
Peach Girl: Poems for a Chinese Daughter
 (with Joan I. Siegel)

CRITICISM

An Aesthetic Toward Notes: On Poets & Poetry

ABOUT THE AUTHOR

Nominated for the National Book Award, the Eric Hoffer Book Award, and nominated three times for the Pulitzer Prize, **J.R. Solonche** is the author of 40 books of poetry and coauthor of another. He lives in the Hudson Valley.

www.ingramcontent.com/pod-product-compliance
Lightning Source LLC
Chambersburg PA
CBHW060535080526
44586CB00012B/742